Inspiring Stories for Amazing Girls
Olivia and the Curious Cloud

Nadia Walker

Inspiring Stories for Amazing Girls:
Olivia and the Curious Cloud
Nadia Walker

Dear Reader,

Thank you for picking up my book!

I created this story to show how even a small act of kindness and love can spread quickly, how working together can create big change, what it means to be a good friend and how powerful believing in yourself is.
I hope you come away after reading this book with a smile on your face and sunshine in your heart.

Nadia Walker
Founder of
Pocket Wisdom Publishing

Contents

The Strange Cloud

In a cute and lively town called Sparkle Junction, nestled in between small green hills and a meadow where colors painted the walls of every building, there was a school named Harmony

Elementary. It was a place where students from all backgrounds came together to learn and play. However, one day something peculiar was happening at Harmony Elementary and in the town of Sparkle Junction.

Meet Olivia, a curious, resourceful, and adventurous girl with a heart as big as the sun. Her best friends are Ethan, Mia, and Noah. They call themselves the Starlight Squad because they love looking up at all the stars at night and dreaming about places they would eventually go and all the adventures they would have.

One day, Olivia noticed a strange occurrence. On this particular sunny afternoon, as she was sitting by her bedroom window looking at a pretty yellow bird on a branch, she noticed a funny, peculiar cloud forming in the sky. It appeared to be unlike any cloud she had ever seen.

Instead of the fluffy cotton ball white shapes she was used to, this cloud had an eerie purple hue and seemed to swirl and shimmer in almost a hypnotic manner. Olivia couldn't take her eyes off it as it slowly drifted closer to her home. Something about this particular cloud made her heart skip a beat.

Intrigued by this unusual cloud, Olivia decided to grab the bird-watching binoculars her grandfather gave her to take a closer look. She zoomed in on the cloud, even though she knew it was miles away. To her surprise, she saw something remarkable. Within the purple mist, there were faint shapes that seemed to resemble beautiful animals and landscapes. "Is that a horse?", "That looks like a dolphin!"

Unable to contain her excitement, Olivia dashed downstairs, "Mom, I'm going over to Mia's! I'll be back before dinner!" "OK honey don't forget your grandfather is coming over at seven. I'm going to make your favorite tacos. Love you! Don't be late!"

The Wonder Woods

Olivia ran next door to Mia's and knocked on the freshly painted but dry red door, bursting to share her discovery with her best friend. As a fellow adventurer of the strange and lover of the unknown, Mia was the perfect person to help her unravel the mystery of the strange cloud.

"You HAVE to tell Ethan and Noah! Noah has been a bit sad lately because his cousin moved away. I think an adventure will cheer him up!" Mia was good that way. She was always the friend who wanted to make sure everyone felt included.

They grabbed their friends Noah and Ethan, and together, the Starlight Squad embarked on a mission to research what could be causing this phenomenon. First, they scoured the internet. Next, they asked Mia's mom, who had read a book every week for the last couple of years. After so much reading, she must know everything!

"That is a strange-looking cloud, but the weather has been so weird for years. It doesn't look threatening. I don't know, guys, it's probably just because of the big changes in weather. Don't worry about it!" Then they asked their neighbor, who was a retired professor. He didn't have an answer and seemed to be very preoccupied with his garden. To their dismay, no one had an explanation for the strange cloud. It seemed as if the cloud showed up randomly out of nowhere, defying all scientific understanding.

Undeterred by their lack of answers, the squad decided to take matters into their own hands. They gathered their hiking gear and set off toward the direction of the cloud. They were determined to get closer to witness this puzzling marvel firsthand.

They hopped on their bikes and followed the strange cloud to a forest.

"I remember being around here before, but I don't remember this forest. Look, there is the bike store right there where my dad brought me to pick out my bike last month!" Noah exclaimed.

"Well, the forest couldn't have appeared out of nowhere," Mia replied.

"Why not? The weird cloud did," Olivia said.

"Clouds can float and move around. This is a forest. Forests don't move around," Ethan said.

Ethan had a good and obvious point. As they trekked through the forest, the world around them seemed to come alive in ways they had never experienced. The air crackled with a certain energy, and the leaves seemed to whisper as they brushed against their skin. A sense of anticipation filled their hearts, and they couldn't shake the feeling that they were being guided toward something extraordinary.

Strange rustling sounds echoed through the trees, and shadows seemed to dance around them. Maybe they should have felt scared, but instead, they felt protected. They felt a mixture of excitement and apprehension, sensing they were on the verge of stepping into a realm unlike anything they had ever known. Their determination remained un-swayed.

Finally, after what felt like an eternity, they reached a clearing where they could see the strange cloud hovering just above the treetops. Its vibrant purple hues left them in awe. As they stood there, so surprised by its beauty, a soft voice broke the silence.

"Welcome," it whispered, weaving through the air like a breeze. They turned to find an old woman standing before them. She had a kind smile and eyes that sparkled with beautiful wisdom.

"I am the Keeper of Dreams," the woman replied.

"I have been watching you closely, Olivia. I sensed your deep curiosity and knew you were special."

Olivia, Mia, Ethan, and Noah exchanged confused and bewildered glances, unsure how this woman knew Olivia's name.

"The cloud you see is a portal to a world of endless possibilities," The Keeper of Dreams continued. "Only those with pure hearts and open minds can witness its magic. You have been chosen."

Olivia's eyes widened with wonder as she realized the magnitude of this encounter. The strange cloud was not just a mere phenomenon; it was a doorway into a hidden world of different possibilities. It existed beyond ordinary reality, where imagination and intention combined with reality.

The Keeper of Dreams explained that this realm, known as Enigma Glade, had been shrouded in secrecy for centuries. It was a place untouched by time, where the beauty of dreams and the power of imagination lived in every corner. Few souls had ever ventured into Enigma Glade.

She told them stories of beautiful creatures that have yet to be seen by human eyes and landscapes so breathtaking they could steal one's breath away. In Enigma Glade, the laws of nature and logic blended with the magical, allowing the intention of its inhabitants to manifest into vivid reality.

But she cautioned them that Glade was not without its challenges. It demanded courage, wisdom, kindness, and unwavering belief in the extraordinary.

"You are going to notice changes in your world. And you are going to lead the change." And at that moment, the forest disappeared, and the Starlight Squad was back in a familiar area of the woods.

"Whaaaaaattt just happened?" "Was that just me, or did you guys see the same thing?" Mia exclaimed.

"Yup!" Noah replied in total shock. They all stood silent for a while.

"What does she even mean? Changes? Chosen for what? Is a good chosen or bad chosen? This can't be real." Olivia yelled out.

"OK, guys, we can't tell anyone about this. No one, I mean absolutely no one would believe this." Ethan said.

"But we ALL saw it. It wasn't like it was just one of us. If all of us saw it, then they would believe something happened." Mia responded.

"No, they could think we just made it up as a prank. Let's just keep this to ourselves. Plus, I don't want my big brother to make fun of me."

They all agreed they wouldn't tell anyone about what they saw.

"I almost forgot! I have to get home for dinner, or my mom will start getting worried!"

Lenticular Clouds

They all set off on their bikes back to town. As they got near Town Square, they noticed a few people whispering and pointing at the sky, and the cloud had moved smack above the center of the town.

As they reached the town park, a small crowd had gathered beneath the shade of the old oak tree. They hopped off their bikes and joined them, eager to find out what was going on.

They listened intently as Mr. Johnson, the town's astronomy enthusiast, shared his theories.

"It's a rare cloud formation known as a lenticular cloud," Mr. Johnson explained, his eyes gleaming with excitement. "They usually form near mountains; it's highly unusual to see one here in Sparkle Junction."

Olivia's curiosity grew stronger by the minute. She thought, "There are more clouds like this? But why aren't they talking about the shimmer and the strange animal formations in the clouds? Or the purple hue? It is so much more magical than they seem to see. Or am I the only person who sees this cloud this way? Is that what she meant by being chosen?"

As the crowd disappeared, Olivia approached Mr. Johnson, her notebook in hand. "Sir, could you tell me more about these lenticular clouds? Why is it so rare to see one over Sparkle Junction?" she asked, her voice brimming with curiosity.

Mr. Johnson smiled warmly at Olivia's enthusiasm. "Well, Olivia, lenticular clouds are typically formed when moist air flows over the mountain range, causing the air to rise, cool, and condense into this very rare and uniquely shaped cloud," he began. "However, our town is located far from any significant mountains, which makes this occurrence quite extraordinary."

"So is that all you SEE?" Olivia asked. "Yes. Otherwise, it looks like a normal cloud to me!" Mr. Johnson replied. "The last time there was mention of a cloud like this was after the great mining accident of Sparkle Junction. A miner named Samuel kept a diary. People were so inspired by his accounts of the events that they published the diary. There should be a copy in the library."

"Oh no! I keep forgetting about dinner! Thank you, Mr. Johnson!" And with that, Olivia, with the rest of the Starlight Squad, went home. But they were determined to unravel the secrets of this enigmatic phenomenon.

Samuel's Diary

The next day, Olivia dug deeper into Sparkle Junction's history. She discovered centuries ago Sparkle Junction had been a thriving mining town. Mines dotted the landscape, with miners working tirelessly beneath the earth's surface. The town flourished, and its people thrived with the abundance of wealth brought by their valuable resources.

However, disaster struck one fateful day when a catastrophic earthquake shook the town. The mountains crumbled, burying the mines and precious resources beneath tons of rubble. Homes were lost, dreams shattered, and Sparkle Junction was forever changed. The once-prosperous town was left wounded and scarred, its spirit broken by the tragedy.

However, Samuel's diary told a different story. His words told a story of resilience and hope. Samuel wrote about how, in the face of adversity, the miners banded together, supporting one another, and rebuilt their lives.

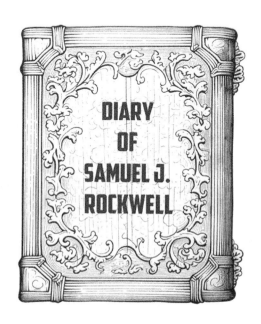

Through Samuel's diary, Olivia discovered that the miners never allowed their spirits to be crushed. With the help of something called the Secret Kindness Club, they used their greatest resource, the sense of community and kindness that bound them together, to transform their shattered town into a place of compassion and caring, where everyone looked out for one another. Interestingly,

Samuel also wrote about a strange and peculiar cloud.

Olivia, Mia, Noah, and Ethan came across old journals dating back to that time, filled with tales of resilience and bravery. The people of Sparkle Junction, though devastated by their losses, refused to let their spirits wane. They were determined to rise above the challenges and rebuild their lives with renewed strength and unity, paving the way to become the beautiful town it is today.

As they poured over these accounts, they began to see a parallel between the cloud and the town's history. The lenticular cloud signaled a beginning of unity and strength that helped embody the spirit of the miners who faced adversity with resilience and kindness.

The Starlight Squad realized the cloud could be a symbol of change and revitalization. Was it a sign that Sparkle Junction was ready to embrace a new chapter of prosperity and communal spirit?

As the days passed, their curiosity grew. They spoke to locals who claimed to have witnessed strange occurrences around the cloud. There were stories of forgotten dreams coming true, acts of kindness multiplying, and a general feeling of goodwill spreading through the town.

Deep inside, Olivia knew the cloud was more than an astronomical phenomenon. It seemed to hold a deeper meaning of something magical and transformative.

Little did she know her curiosity would lead her on a remarkable journey of self-discovery, love, and friendship. As she delved deeper into the mystery of the cloud, Olivia learned the power of kindness and the extraordinary impact it could have on an entire community.

The Secret Kindness Club

Olivia, while doing some research in the library, came upon an old, faded newspaper article from years ago, again mentioning something called the Secret Kindness Club. The article mentioned the Secret Kindness Club was a group of individuals who sought to spread kindness in the world anonymously. Their members would perform small acts of kindness without seeking recognition or praise. The club's sole purpose was to make the world a better place, one act of kindness at a time.

"They sound really cool! Making people feel happy. I love that!" Olivia exclaimed.

"Me too!" Ethan, Mia, and Noah said in unison.

The Starlight's squad's curiosity turned into admiration, and a spark of inspiration ignited them. They knew they had stumbled upon something truly special. They all promised to find a way, if it was possible, to become part of this Secret Kindness Club, to make a real difference in their school and community with others who shared the same values. Did The Secret Kindness Club still exist?

Little did this band of adventurers know that the Secret Kindness Club did still indeed exist but also had a unique initiation process. It wasn't just anyone who could join; one needed to prove their commitment to kindness and prove their willingness to help others.

Even though the Starlight Squad wasn't sure if the club still existed, they were still ready to take on the challenge of genuinely making a difference.

Over the next few weeks, they began performing small acts of kindness throughout the town. Mia helped an elderly man with his groceries at the market. Ethan donated his time at the community center putting things away, and Olivia left anonymous notes of encouragement for her classmates. Noah went throughout the neighborhood to see if he could help with yard work. Even if they weren't getting errand money, they were happy knowing they were making a difference, just like the members of the Secret Kindness Club.

As the group continued their quest to join the club, they heard whispers and rumors from her classmates about mysterious acts of kindness happening around them. Some had found encouraging notes, and others have received unexpected help when they needed it, often hidden. But there were lots of additional acts of kindness the Starlight Squad knew they weren't responsible for. Someone else was out there, too, spreading kindness in their community. Were their helpful gestures growing?

With each act of kindness, Olivia could feel herself growing closer to the Secret Kindness Club. Little did she know, the club was watching her, silently observing her dedication. They had been waiting for someone like Olivia and her friends, those people who would go above and beyond to make the world a little bit brighter.

One day, as Olivia returned home after yet another act of kindness, she found a small envelope with her name on it. Inside was a handwritten note that read,

"Congratulations, Olivia. You have proven your capacity for true kindness. We have been watching your every move, and it is with great pleasure we invite you to join us in the Secret Kindness Club."

Olivia was so excited she called her best friends right away. "We got the same note!! They are real! We all made it!" Excitement bubbled within Olivia's heart as she reread the note. She and her best friends were now embarking on another glorious adventure!

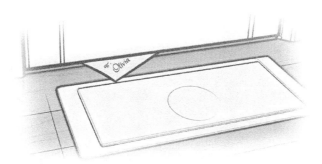

The Secret Kindness Club had noticed her and her friends' efforts, and now they were beckoning them

to join them on their journey to spread kindness. Along with the note, there was a map leading to a hidden location where the club held its meetings.

With newfound determination, the group grabbed their essentials kit complete with flashlight, phone charger, tracker, compass and snacks and followed the map along through paths and forests until they reached a clearing where a beautiful cabin stood.

The cabin exuded an aura of warmth and compassion, nestled in the arms of nature.

A Tribe of Purpose

They all stood outside hesitantly. "Noah, you gave your brother a copy of the map and told him where we were going right?". Noah nodded. "Everyone told someone right?" Olivia asked looking at the rest of the group. They all nodded.

"Olivia, you go first, you are the leader of this whole thing," Ethan pointed out.

Olivia took a deep breath and cautiously entered the cabin, her heart pounding with anticipation and she was enveloped by a sense of belonging as she took her first step through the door. In a golden-lit room, she saw a group of people sitting in a circle, their faces glowing with smiles. The members welcomed Olivia and her friends with open arms, recognizing them for their commitment to spreading kindness.

They explained the Secret Kindness Club was founded by a group of best friends just like them a long time ago, who had witnessed the power of small acts of kindness.

Each member had their own story and their own experiences that had brought them to the realization that the world needed more good deeds and love. They each saw how a single kind gesture could pick up someone's day, and they realized the big potential for change if more people joined their cause.

The room was filled with people from all walks of life, each armed with their own unique talent or skill to contribute. There were musicians, writers, doctors, business leaders... young and old.

Inside the cabin, the members shared their stories of kindness endeavors, inspiring one another with stories of lives touched, burdens lifted, and communities united. They exchanged ideas, discussed projects, and made plans for future acts of kindness. In this circle of like-minded people, the Starlight Squad felt an overwhelming sense of belonging and purpose.

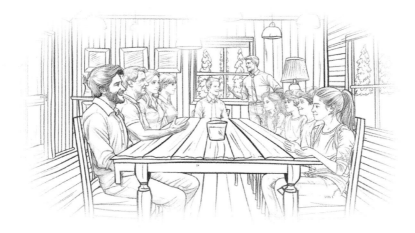

The Secret Kindness Club wasn't just a group of people, it felt like a family united by a shared purpose. They promised to continue dedicating their lives to spreading kindness even during tough times, knowing their actions had the power to shape the world. They supported one another, offering guidance, encouragement, and a shoulder to lean on during challenging times.

In that cabin, surrounded by the Secret Kindness Club's members, Olivia realized they weren't just changing the world; they were changing themselves, too. The acts of kindness were not only impacting those on the receiving end but were changing the hearts and minds of the club's members as well. Olivia felt honored to be part of this extraordinary group, knowing she had found her purpose and her tribe. As Noah, Mia, Ethan, and Olivia went back to their daily routine, chatter started to grow about random acts of kindness all over the town.

Harmony Elementary

Olivia couldn't contain her excitement as she sat down at the desk, ready to embark on her mission to spread good vibes throughout the school. She knew that the Kindness Club had already made a difference to her and her friends, but she wanted to take it to the next level.

With a determined smile on her face, Olivia started brainstorming ideas to spread the word. She started leaving cheerful notes in lockers and organized surprise recess games. She even decided to create a "Kindness Corner" where new or shy kids can sign up and the Starlight Squad would introduce themselves and show them around the school or play games with them.

Olivia remembered when Noah first came to school from California and didn't know anyone. She was the first one to go up and say hi to Noah. Noah later said he was so happy and relieved when she came up and introduced herself to him.

He felt really alone being the new kid at school and not having any friends yet.

Looking back, Olivia was so glad she started talking to Noah that first day. Now he is one of her very best friends and they have been on so many adventures together. This might not have happened if she hadn't introduced herself first! She always remembered this, so she wanted anyone who was shy or new to always have a friend in her and her squad.

Olivia also decided to create colorful posters with uplifting quotes and messages. She wanted the posters to serve as daily reminders for students to be nice to each other.

She again enlisted the help of her best friends, and together, they spent hours cutting out letters, drawing positive illustrations, and carefully decorating posters.

Once the posters were ready, Olivia thought about perfect places to hang them. She wanted them to be in areas where students would see them every day. After careful consideration, she chose the hallways, the cafeteria, the library, and even the bathroom stalls and detention hall.

"The detention hall is a great idea. No one likes being stuck there." Noah replied.

She believed the kindness posters shouldn't be limited to certain places. It should be everywhere, even in the most unexpected corners of the school.

Olivia also knew that students could be oblivious to their surroundings, especially when they were busy chatting with friends, looking at their phones or rushing to their next class. She needed a way to capture their attention and make them stop and really absorb the message.

"Any other ideas besties? I think we can do more." They all shrugged.

The Kindness Challenge

As Olivia walked into her house, she smelled cake in the air! "That's right! It's Dad's birthday today!" She was thankful her mom reminded her last week. That gave her enough time to make her dad a handmade heart card and buy him his favorite golf balls.

Both the slightly crinkled card and the perfectly wrapped box were hiding under her bed, so her dad wouldn't see them before the big day.

As she passed in the kitchen, she saw a postcard marked "Happy Birthday" from her grandmother.

"That's it! I know what we can do next! "

At that moment, Olivia came up with the idea of creating the Kindness Challenge. She printed out small cards with prompts like "Compliment a stranger", "Help someone carry their books", "Listen attentively to a friend", and "Write a kind note to a classmate". Each card had the hashtag

#SpreadKindness printed on it. Olivia hoped that this will not only motivate them to practice kindness but also inspire others who see their social media posts.

Olivia challenged her classmates to fulfill at least one act of kindness every day and if they wanted to... post about it, explaining they would not only be spreading "happy energy" within their school but also to the larger online community.

She reminded them of the incredible power of their actions and how they could touch the lives of people they had never even met. Olivia's heart grew bigger just thinking about it.

As the days passed, Olivia noticed a change in the school's atmosphere. People were smiling more, offering help without being asked, and creating an environment of compassion and empathy. Students who were initially hesitant had now started to participate in the kindness challenge whole-heartedly. The posters caught everyone's attention with their bright colors and beautiful messages. Not only were they fulfilling the challenges, but they were also coming up with their own creative acts of kindness.

Students who previously passed each other without saying a word now shared genuine smiles. Friendships bloomed among unlikely people, bridging gaps that seemed wide before. Olivia couldn't be prouder of her school, and she knew this was just the beginning.

Students, teachers, and even teachers shared with Olivia, her best friends, and her family the powerful messages of thanks for the positive changes they had witnessed. Stories of how small acts of kindness had turned someone's day around or built expected friendships filled her heart with joy. The Starlight Squad, led by Olivia, was now reaching into the community just as she had hoped. By spreading the word and inspiring others, she started to create a ripple effect that would extend far beyond their school.

She saw changes at home. One afternoon at home, she heard her mom on the phone. She sounded upset.

All she heard was, "Oh no! I can't believe it. Is she OK? Please call me if you hear anything else." Olivia peered around the corner past the blue flower wallpaper in the hallway and saw her mom just sit down and put her head on the table.

Olivia later asked her dad, "Is Mommy OK? She seemed sad when she got off the phone."

Her dad replied, "Mommy's friend is in the hospital, so she is really worried. I'm sure she will be all right."

Olivia went up to her mom and asked, "Mommy, I am sorry to hear about your friend. Daddy told me. I want to help you. Can I help you with the dishes this week?"

Her Mom replied, "Thank you, my darling girl. Thank you for thinking of me. How about we do the dishes together? That will cheer me up."

Olivia was happy to spend time with her mom AND help. She noticed her younger brother, Charlie, joined in on the "helper" bandwagon, too. Most days, he tried to annoy her. This day, he asked if she would like help setting the table.

Her dad said, "I think you are having a good influence on him. I am proud of you," and smiled.

Not only was Olivia being an example at school but at home too. She knew kindness isn't just a concept but a powerful force that could bring people together, uplift people, and create lasting connections.

As Olivia went to bed that night, she looked out the window. She looked up at where the peculiar cloud used to be and saw a shimmery golden outline of the wise woman in the woods. She seemed to be looking down and smiling. Olivia rubbed her eyes, but when she looked back up, the shimmery outline was gone.

Just then, Olivia then got an even bigger plan to spread kindness beyond her small community.

The next day, she called her friends together at lunch, plopped down her plate of mac and cheese, and said, "I have an idea. Let's have a party! We are going to call it the Kindness Carnival!

The Adventure Architects

The following Sunday afternoon, the Starlight Squad gathered in their tree house. The air was filled with determination.

Olivia said, "Guys, we need something big. A place filled with games, activities, and challenges that encourage kindness but also make it tons of fun! So, it's not just about kindness. It's a celebration of it." The group started sketching the big idea on a large cardboard piece on the floor with a bright red marker.

The plan started to take shape. Ethan would take care of the booths, and Mia, with her artistic flair, spearheaded the artwork, starting with the "Kindness Art Wall" at the entrance, turning a white dull wall into a bright display of light, beauty, and color. Noah and Olivia worked on the rest of the details, making sure everything would run smoothly.

As the Starlight Squad delved deeper into their planning, the excitement in the treehouse grew palpable. The sun cast a warm glow through the windows, casting a sense of camaraderie and purpose among the friends.

Mia, fueled by her artistic passion, set to work on transforming the school's recess entrance wall into a masterpiece. She envisioned a mural full of brightness and joy. Mia's brushstrokes would bring to life a scene showing people helping each other, spreading smiles, and making the community a beautiful place.

Noah and Olivia worked on making sure everything ran smoothly. They discussed the schedule, the flow of activities, and back up plans in case anything went wrong. Olivia emphasized the importance of celebrating the good in your life and turning the event into a very memorable experience for all attendees.

Ethan, with his organizational skills, began brainstorming various booth ideas. He envisioned a "Compassion Cafe " where people could buy the most delicious food, and each treat would contain a heartfelt message written by the children of the school.

The "Challenge Zone" with interactive games that promoted teamwork and cooperation, and the "Acts of Kindness Emporium " would be a big space where people could explore their creativity with a variety of crafts to bring their creative visions to life. The rest of the Starlight Squad started throwing out so many great ideas he couldn't write them down fast enough. "How about a storytelling tent!" "What about a time capsule!", "How about we throw in some dancing and music?"

Ethan, at one point, threw up his hands. "Slow down! One at a time. These ideas are amazing, but I'm not a machine!"

Then they all at once, they looked at each other and started laughing. Olivia even got up and did a little dance. "Wow! I can't believe this is really happening!"

The team continued to refine their plans, incorporating more ideas to make the event truly magical.

They also discussed talking to local businesses and community members to make the event a team effort that brought the whole town together.

With each passing moment, the tree house buzzed with anticipation of the upcoming kindness celebration. The Starlight Squad's determination and creativity were boundless, and they were well on their way to turning their dream into a reality.

As the sun dipped lower in the sky, the tree house echoed with laughter, the rustle of marker pens, and the hum of creative energy. The Starlight Squad was on a mission to create an event that would not only be entertaining but also leave a lasting impact on their community.

Teamwork With The Tall Helpers: The Grown-ups

In the bustling halls of Harmony Elementary, Olivia felt a burst of excitement bubbling within her. With her eyes sparkling like stars, she approached the wise and warm-hearted Principal Evans, whose office was filled with sunlight filtering through colorful children's drawings adorning the walls. Olivia couldn't wait to share her grand plan for something extraordinary – The Kindness Carnival.

"Hi, Principal Evans!" Olivia greeted him with a beaming smile, her enthusiasm contagious.

Principal Evans, a pillar of support for the school community, looked up from his desk, his eyes meeting Olivia's. "Hello, Olivia! What brings you here today?"

With a skip in her step, Olivia dove into her vision of The Kindness Carnival, painting a clear picture of a day filled with laughter, joy, and acts of kindness that would ripple through the entire school and beyond. Principal Evans listened attentively, captivated by Olivia's passion and the potential for positivity.

As Olivia spoke, Principal Evans couldn't help but notice the big transformation the Acts of Kindness movement had already brought to the school. He saw how simple, yet powerful acts of empathy had created a tapestry of connection among students and staff. The sometimes-chaotic hallways now echoed with laughter, and quiet friendships blossomed.

At that moment, Principal Evans, recognizing the genuine impact of Olivia's vision, decided to become not just a spectator but an active participant in making The Kindness Carnival a reality. "Olivia," he said with a nod and a warm smile, "I believe in your vision. Let's make The Kindness Carnival something truly special for everyone."

Olivia's eyes widened with joy, grateful for the unwavering support from Principal Evans. "Thank you so much, Principal Evans! This is going to be amazing!"

With Principal Evans fully on board, Olivia knew that to turn her vision into reality, she needed a team of dedicated volunteers. She took the initiative to contact the school paper. The call for volunteers inspired students who were excited to be part of something so unique and special.

And so, with Principal Evans by her side and a team of enthusiastic volunteers ready to bring The Kindness Carnival to life, Olivia's vision was set in motion, creating a wave of anticipation and goodwill that enveloped the entire school. The journey toward The Kindness Carnival had begun, and every step carried the vision of turning dreams into a day filled with kindness, connection, and joy.

Armed with cool bright posters, they strategically placed them around the school, creating a buzz of anticipation among their fellow students.

The news of the Kindness Carnival didn't stop there at the school; the chatter spread through the town, catching the attention of local media outlets. The excitement reached its peak when a local TV crew decided to cover the event, turning the Kindness Carnival into a widely anticipated affair.

The Starlight Squad's mission to recruit local businesses and leaders also began with "Operation Kidpreneur". The group would go door to door and ask for help from the town's largest businesses to contribute to The Kindness Carnival cause.

Olivia said, "Local businesses can sponsor specific activities or booths, and we can give them special recognition during the event. It's a win-win! Who doesn't want to support kids?" She was right. With the help of their parents, the students, Principal Evans and the local businesses, Olivia and her besties were able to receive all the resources they needed to make their vision come to life.

Mrs. Mason's local bakery was able to make the cakes, cookies, and other delicious treats for the "Compassion Cafe".

Mr. Webster donated all the building materials for the event and volunteered his college sons home from a break to help create the structures. One of the sons, Raphael, showed the structure he had built for an event in the desert called "Burning Man". The structure was so big but looked really strange.

Noah asked, "What's that for?"

"It's art", Raph replied.

"It is? I guess I don't understand art". Noah shrugged.

"That's OK, small fry. You will one day!" Raph laughed.

"Well, OK". Noah wasn't so sure, but he was grateful to have their help anyway. He knew this was such a big task, and they couldn't do this without getting a lot of grown-ups involved.

The president of the local community bank, Mrs. Ellie, helped fund most of the costs. Her daughter, Sophie, was very shy, and Olivia and her friends befriended her when she walked into the "Kindness Corner". Mrs. Ellie saw the difference the new group of friends made in Sophie's confidence and was moved to help however she could.

As the energy extended well beyond the tight-knit circle of the Starlight Squad to the rest of Harmony Elementary, the students enthusiastically rallied together to cover the remaining costs of the carnival. Their weekends transformed into a flurry of soapy suds and cheerful chatter as they organized car wash fundraisers. The school's parking lot became a colorful spectacle with buckets, sponges, and energetic children armed with spray hoses. The students took pride in their efforts, and the car washes turned into mini-festivals themselves, complete with homemade cupcakes, laughter, and an overwhelming sense of accomplishment for the students who, through their collective efforts, became an important part of the magical journey unfolding in their school and beyond.

This Kindness Carnival was all coming together.

From Dreams to Reality: The Big Day

Then, finally, as the sun rose on a crisp autumn morning, the town was abuzz with excitement. The months of planning and preparation had led up to this very day. Olivia, her group of besties, Ethan, Noah and Mia, the school, the town and even their friends from the Secret Kindness Club, had turned their idea into a reality. The Kindness Carnival.

The playground had been transformed into a magical wonderland. Bright colors with messages of kindness fluttered in the wind, and colorful booths were set up for various activities aimed and spreading joy, happiness, and fun!

Olivia couldn't help but feel a surge of pride as she looked over the carnival grounds.

They had managed to unite the community under one purpose, demonstrating the power of collective action. What had started as a small group of friends was now a movement that captured the hearts of the whole town.

The cobbled paths of the carnival were lined with beautifully crafted booths, each one representing a different aspect of kindness. At the "Compassion Cafe", volunteers served warm cups of cocoa and delicious freshly made treats, taking the time to engage in heartfelt conversations with anyone who needed someone to listen to them. They poured love and compassion into each interaction, creating a comforting place for those burdened by any worries. A sense of belonging swirled throughout the cafe, leaving visitors with a warm feeling in their hearts and renewed belief in themselves.

Sitting nearby was the "Adventures in Gratitude" booth, a collaborative effort put together by the children of the school and adults alike. Here, visitors were encouraged to write down the things they were grateful for on brightly colored leaves and attach them to a beautiful gratitude tree. The branches of the tree sagged under the weight of gratitude and appreciation, creating a visual representation of the abundance of good in their lives. People stopped and paused in reflection, realizing the many simple joys that often went unnoticed, like the warm sun, flowers, rain, a simple apple, or a nice cozy bath. The booth became a reminder to cherish everyday moments and express gratitude for the good that surrounded them.

Sometimes, Olivia felt like she was running around so much she forgot to take a moment to appreciate everything she had. Sure, some things could have been better in her life, but if you focus on just the bad, you can often miss the good. She took a moment right there to be thankful for her mom, her dad, her grandparents, her besties, her home, her school and even her sometimes annoying brother. And she didn't forget the magical wise woman she met in the woods wherever she was and the strange cloud!

The sound of laughter drew Olivia's attention to another booth called "Positive Vibes Only". Here, a group of comedians and improv artists showcased their talents to make people belly laugh. They helped everyone see the lighter side of life. The contagious laughter echoed throughout the carnival, erasing daily frustrations, and filling the air with joy. Visitors found themselves carrying laughter within them long after they had left the carnival grounds.

Her mom told her that laughter is healthy, so she definitely wanted to have a booth at the Carnival that made people really laugh.

Further down the path stood the "Acts of Kindness Emporium". Volunteers had transformed it into an amazing space filled with cool crafts and DIY projects, each aimed at inspiring visitors to think creatively about how they could make a positive impact in someone's life. Children busily created kindness jars and handmade cards, imagining the smile that their efforts would bring to someone else. The emporium became a hub of ideas and inspiration. There were even the "Joyful Jugglers of Good Deeds" around the emporium, showcasing their juggling skills but with a twist. Instead of traditional juggling balls, they skillfully tossed and caught tiny representations of dreams like hearts and stars.

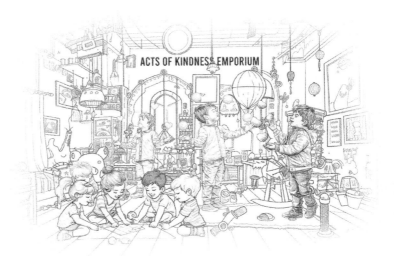

Next up was the "Compliment Carousel". Ethan, the ingenious architect of the Compliment Carousel, created the booth with an inventive spirit. With each spin of the carousel, the unveiling of compliments became an interactive wonder – not just giving you a compliment but releasing an explosion of sparkling confetti at the same time. Then, a fun tune danced through the air. It transformed compliment receiving into a multi-sensory celebration. She saw her mom smile when the carousel yelled, "You are beautiful!" and then splashed rainbow confetti from the sky. Mia and Olivia laughed later that they woke up the next morning with shiny confetti on their pillow from their hair even though they had taken a shower the night before.

Then, in the middle of all this, a surprise flash mob emerged, choreographed by the dance teacher, Mrs. Alina, to an energetic song about believing in yourself. The flash mob got even bigger and more fun as students from all grades spontaneously joined in, showing off their dance moves. The "Dance of Unity Flash Mob" impromptu performance became a surprise highlight of the day, turning the carnival into an instant dance party.

The big structure in the middle was the "Magic of Connection Tent". Inside, storytellers captivated the audience with stories of courage, compassion, and love. In addition, the members of the Kindness Club all took turns telling stories about their most interesting encounters. People of all ages sat cross-legged, riveted by the experiences. It was here that the true spirit of the carnival blossomed, creating bonds that transcended age, culture, and background. Through these stories, people discovered the common threads that wove their lives together and how much they had in common with each other. They listened to stories that taught them empathy, inspired them to see beyond their own experiences, and encouraged them to embrace the power of connection in their own lives.

The Starlight Squad also told some of their most recent stories. One was about Mrs. Thompson, a neighbor who had been feeling a bit lonely. They decided to bring some joy into her day by creating a "Smile Mender" kit. Filled with drawings, jokes, and little surprises, the kit worked like magic.

Mrs. Thompson's frown turned upside down, showing everyone that little acts of kindness can truly mend smiles.

Another story was about Mr. and Mrs. Baker, an elderly couple who missed the music they used to dance to in their younger days. Olivia, with the help of the music teacher, organized a surprise "House of Hearts" concert. Local musicians played the couple's favorite tunes, turning their backyard into a mini dance floor. Tears of joy flowed as the Bakers danced, rediscovering the melody of their love through the ingenuity of their young friends.

At the carnival, Noah and Mia went around carrying the "Generosity Grab Bag" and randomly giving them to the students. In the grab bag were surprise tokens that entitled them to unique acts of kindness. Some found tickets for a day off from homework that they coordinated with the teachers, while others received invitations to a "Secret Lunch Party" hosted by the Starlight Squad. The anticipation added an element of fun surprise to the carnival. Olivia was particularly happy that a new girl at school picked an invite token to the lunch party. She remembered how Noah felt when he was new to the school, so she was looking forward to meeting a possible new friend.

At the edge of the carnival, near a wooded area, there was a garden. Olivia remembered her mom saying there is a lot of power in people thinking the same thought, so she decided to add a "Vision Garden." It was a space where people could plant seeds, symbolizing the growth of positive actions. Mia's artistic touch extended to this corner, where she had painted murals of blooming flowers, each petal had a positive word on it.

The centerpiece of the garden was a uniquely crafted planting station, where people could select seeds representing different uplifting actions... from tiny seeds of a compliment to the growing potential of a charitable gesture. The variety was as diverse as the ways a person could spread thoughtfulness... cute pots decorated with affirmations and encouraging messages waited their turn to grow these seeds of positivity.

The air carried the gritty earthy scent of soil as young and old hands alike planted their chosen seeds. The act of planting became a symbolic commitment to nurture love in their own lives and watch it bloom into something beautiful over time.

The Vision Garden wasn't just a display; it was an interactive experience that encouraged people to reflect on the impact of their actions. Surrounding the planting station were inspirational stories of real-life acts of caring, providing a stream of motivation for those eager to contribute to the growing garden of positivity.

As the sun cast its golden glow over the garden, it became a living symbol to the group effort of a community determined to plant seeds of kindness.

Next was Ethan's favorite, "The Challenge Zone". This booth was thoughtfully designed by Ethan to be a kaleidoscope of interactive games to not only have fun but also created a vibe of teamwork and cooperation.

The "Puzzle Pyramid" was a three-dimensional challenge requiring teams to solve puzzles to find a hidden message. The sound of puzzle pieces clicking into place echoed the satisfaction of team problem-solving, supporting the idea that working together could unravel even the hardest challenges. Or the "Team Trails"- timed activities that needed coordinated effort. Whether it was moving through a maze blindfolded or working together in a fast-paced relay race, these trials showed the importance of teamwork in overcoming obstacles.

The air was filled with cheers and encouraging shouts as participants triumphed over each challenge. The Challenge Zone wasn't just a collection of games; it was a living example of the Starlight Squad's vision – a place where people learned that through cooperation, they could achieve far more than they ever could alone.

The last structure was the "Kindness Time Capsule" Booth. Carnival goers wrote letters to their future selves, storing memories of today's events, the lessons they learned, and their hopes for the future. The letters were sealed in a time capsule to be opened by their future selves exactly ten years from today. Olivia thought hard and took a snapshot in her mind of today and wished for her future self to remember this day always. And to always believe in herself. She and her small band of adventurers were indeed able to change the whole town. She wondered what the rest of her friends put in that capsule.

On the way out, each person was to drop something in the big "Whimsical Wish Jar". They could write down their deepest wishes for themselves and the world and place them in the jar. Everyone seemed protective of their dreams, and they went to a place to think and scribble before they dropped their note into the jar.

Once in a while, Olivia would hear Noah yell, "We need more pencils! I think people are taking them for good luck because we keep running out!" It is a good thing she coordinated with the art department to make sure they were stocked with enough engraved "Kindness Carnival" pencils.

At the end of the day, the jar was filled to the brim with dreams of creating a picture of all the wishes for the future.

As the day progressed, the joy of the Kindness Carnival continued to spread. Friendships blossomed, neighbors reconnected, and strangers found comfort in the support of the community. The carnival had created a tapestry of love, celebrating the best that is within all of us. As dusk settled in, Olivia stood at the center of the carnival, the heartbeat of gratitude surrounded her. Looking out at the crowds, she couldn't help feeling truly fulfilled. The Kindness Carnival had been transformative, not just for the town but for herself and her friends as well.

With the carnival drawing to a close, Olivia and her friends felt a mix of emotions—joy for the success they had achieved, appreciation for the community that had supported their vision, and a strong sense of hope for the future. Though the carnival would soon fade into beautiful memories, its impact would live on in the hearts and actions of those who had witnessed its magic. And they were all VERY thankful it didn't rain.

As the sun set on this extraordinary day, the Kindness Carnival embraced its final moments.

The world around them seemed to shift as if acknowledging the transformative power of connections.

The Next Level: The Kindness Nation

In the weeks that followed the Kindness Carnival, Olivia received countless letters and calls from people in the community, sharing how the event had impacted them. Parents wrote about how their children had started showing more compassion towards their siblings and friends, while students shared stories of reaching out to their classmates who were struggling. Teachers spoke of a renewed sense of positivity and cooperation in their classrooms.

Word of the Starlight Squad's extraordinary carnival, filled with kindness and community spirit, reached the ears of a local journalist eager to uncover the inspiration behind this magical event. Olivia, ever humble and eager to share the spotlight with her friends, invited the journalist to their tree house, a place that had become the center of their creative adventures.

As the journalist settled into the cozy tree house surrounded by sketches, plans, and the contagious enthusiasm of the Starlight Squad, Olivia welcomed the opportunity to share their journey. "We're really just a group of friends who wanted to spread a little joy in our community," she began, waving for her friends to join in.

Noah, clearing his throat to sound practical, chimed in, "We started by thinking about what would make people happy, and that's how the idea of a kindness carnival got started. Something that celebrated the power of caring and bringing people together."

Ethan, part of the organizational brain behind the booths, added, "But we knew we couldn't do it alone. That's when the idea of involving local businesses and community members came up. It wasn't just about organizing an event; it was about creating something that really lifted the community's spirit."

The journalist turned to Mia, the artistic soul of the group, "Mia, tell me about the 'Kindness Art Wall' and your idea for switching up the entrance."

Mia's eyes sparkled, "I wanted to create pictures that immediately brightened people's day when they walked in... almost like starting a happy journey.

The wall was a symbol of how kindness can change even the simplest of things."

Even Olivia's little brother Charlie chimed in. Filled with lots of energy, waiting for the moment to share his thoughts, "And we wanted everyone to feel like superheroes! Everyone can be a hero, even if it's just for a day." Everyone laughed as he pranced around the tree house with his cape made of his old blue baby blanket. Some days, Olivia found her brother annoying, but now, most days, she just found him absolutely adorable. She looked forward to when he got older, and he would not only be her little brother but become a fellow adventurer and close friend.

The journalist turned to Olivia, "I can't believe what you guys have built! It's incredible. And what about your vision for involving so many different groups of people?" Olivia nodded, "We wanted this event to be a true town effort. We couldn't have done it without our parents, the school, and the local businesses. But it's not just about the event day. It's about building lasting connections within our community."

As they continued sharing their story, each member of the Starlight Squad spoke from the heart. They touched on the challenges they initially faced and the joy of witnessing the event come to life. Noah spoke about the logistical hurdles, Mia shared the emotional journey of creating the art installations, and Ethan described the excitement of seeing the whole town have fun together.

In the midst of their shared story, the journalist couldn't help but be captivated by the realness and passion in their voices. It was a story not just of a carnival but of a community coming together, of friendships deepening, and of kindness leaving a mark on the hearts of all involved.

As the interview concluded, Olivia looked around at her friends, their eyes shining with a shared sense of accomplishment. The tree house, once a simple hangout place, had become a statement to the power of friendship, creativity, and the big impact of spreading kindness in their community.

The influence of the Kindness Carnival continued to grow over time. Other schools in the district heard about its success and started organizing their own versions of the event. The movement became a bigger movement called "The Kindness Nation", and it spread like wildfire, with compassionate initiatives popping up in communities far and wide.

Neighboring schools looked to have similar programs to create unity and empathy among their own students. The larger community also witnessed the transformation and saw the effect it had on the whole town. The spirit of collaboration and kindness was recycled just like during the Sparkle Junction mining accident but renewed in a much bigger, wider way.

As the students matured and moved on to higher grades, they took the spirit of kindness with them. Their influence spread to middle schools, high schools, and eventually to universities and workplaces. The ripple of change, which had originated from the cloud that so mysteriously formed above their town, had transformed into a tidal wave of compassion, touching countless lives along the way. Little did this tiny band of curious, imaginative best friends know that their magical event would not only inspire kindness but also become a cherished tradition in their community and beyond for years to come.

And so, the journey of Harmony Elementary was not just a remarkable story but a timeless lesson in compassion, empathy, and the ability of every individual to change the world. As the students grew up and looked back on their journey, they felt an immense sense of pride, knowing that their small acts of kindness had ignited a revolution of love and understanding. They held onto the hope that this revolution would continue to flourish, creating a more compassionate and harmonious world for all.

And all this started with a little curious adventurous girl with a big heart following a strange peculiar purple hued shimmery cloud on a sunny afternoon...

HARMONY ELEMENTARY REUNION

The End

What are some of the lessons you learned from this book?

Write down some of your thoughts on the following pages

KINDNESS IS LIKE A RIPPLE!

WHEN YOU TOSS A PEBBLE INTO A POND,
THE RIPPLE SPREADS OUT FAR AND WIDE.

_____
_____
_____
_____
_____
_____
_____
_____
_____
_____
_____
_____
_____
_____
_____
_____
_____
_____
_____
_____

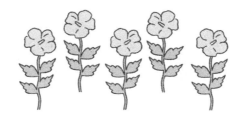

ASK FOR HELP WHEN YOU NEED IT!

EVERYONE NEEDS HELP SOMETIMES.
IT'S BRAVE TO ASK FOR HELP
WHEN YOU NEED IT.

_____
_____
_____
_____
_____
_____
_____
_____
_____
_____
_____
_____
_____
_____
_____
_____
_____
_____

TEAMWORK IS POWERFUL

WORKING TOGETHER IS LIKE BUILDING A GIANT PUZZLE. EACH PIECE IS IMPORTANT AND TOGETHER CAN CREATE AMAZING THINGS!

_____

_____

_____

_____

_____

_____

_____

_____

_____

_____

_____

_____

_____

_____

_____

_____

_____

_____

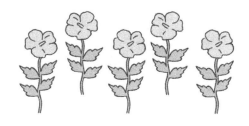

YOU CAN DO SO MUCH WHEN YOU BELIEVE IN YOURSELF!

GIVE YOUR BEST EFFORTS AND BELIEVE IN YOURSELF. YOU CAN DO MORE THAN YOU REALIZE.

_____
_____
_____
_____
_____
_____
_____
_____
_____
_____
_____
_____
_____
_____
_____
_____
_____
_____

BE A GOOD FRIEND

A GOOD FRIEND LISTENS, SHARES, AND
UNDERSTANDS. HELP WHEN OTHERS
STUMBLE AND CHEER WHEN THEY SUCCEED.

_____
_____
_____
_____
_____
_____
_____
_____
_____
_____
_____
_____
_____
_____
_____
_____
_____
_____
_____
_____
_____

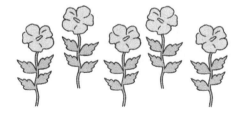

BE YOUR UNIQUE SELF

SHINE YOUR STAR IN YOUR OWN UNIQUE WAY. BE PROUD OF WHAT MAKES YOU DIFFERENT. IT'S YOUR OWN SPECIAL MAGIC THAT NO ONE ELSE HAS.

BE GRATEFUL FOR THE GOOD

LIFE ISN'T GOING TO BE PERFECT AND
THINGS CAN GO WRONG OR BE UNFAIR.
REMEMBER ALL THE GOOD THINGS
AROUND YOU BIG AND SMALL.

_____
_____
_____
_____
_____
_____
_____
_____
_____
_____
_____
_____
_____
_____
_____
_____
_____
_____
_____
_____
_____

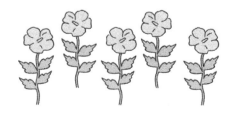

ALWAYS REMEMBER

YOU ARE BEAUTIFUL

YOU ARE BRAVE

YOU ARE SMART

YOU ARE AMAZING

SHINE YOUR LIGHT!

IF YOU LIKED READING

OLIVIA

AND THE CURIOUS CLOUD

WE WOULD LOVE

IF YOU LEFT US A REVIEW

IF YOU HAVE ANY QUESTIONS

OR COMMENTS

YOU CAN REACH OUT TO

NADIA@POCKETWISDOMCOMPANY.COM

Made in the USA
Monee, IL
16 March 2025

14090299R00046